DISCARD

The Back Road to Arcadia

Michael Heffernan

The Back Road to Arcadia

SALMON POETRY

Published in 1994 by
Salmon Publishing Ltd,
Upper Fairhill, Galway
A division of Poolbeg Enterprises Ltd

The Publishers gratefully acknowledge the assistance of The Arts Council

The moral right of the author has been asserted.

A catalogue record for this book is available from the British Library.

ISBN 1 897648 01 4

Cover illustration by Sue Smickler
Cover design by Poolbeg Group Services Ltd
Set by Poolbeg Group Services Ltd in Palatino 10.5/14
Printed by Colour Books, Baldoyle Industrial Estate, Dublin 13

Acknowledgements

The author thanks the editors of the following journals where these poems first appeared, sometimes in earlier versions:

The American Poetry Review "A Canticle of the Stars"

The Chariton Review "The Monks at Large"

Cyphers (Ireland) "The Abyss" and "The Atonement"

The Gettysburg Review "The Atonement," "Badia Fiesolana," "The Light of the Living," "Truth," and "Watering Impatiens"

The Iowa Review "Angelology," "Lawn Mower," and "A Light in the House"

Kentucky Poetry Review "Merciless Beauty"

The New Criterion "Magpies" and "The World of Light"

The Quarterly "The Ape of Emain Macha," "The Banquet," "The Flesh," "A Highway Brook in Dingle," "The Land of Heart's Desire," "Lost Boy," "The Nightgown," "The Peasants' Rising," "The Queen of Heaven," "The Rooming House," and "Summer in Umbria"

Shenandoah "A Catch in the Breath," "A Girl Sings to Moravia at the World's End," and "The Moving Statue at Melleray"

Willow Springs "Café Paradiso," "The Music of Forgiveness," and "Requiem"

This book's completion was assisted by fellowship grants from the National Endowment for the Arts, the Arkansas Arts Council, and An Chomhairle Ealaíon/The Arts Council, Ireland.

Contents

The Abyss

A monk rowed out to sea in a boat no bigger
than the pallet he left behind in his tiny cell.
Light as a wafer it wobbled over the waves.
The box with his belongings had lost its lid
and left his wake awash with loveletters.
Just beyond sight of land he raised the oars
and crossed them at his feet and said his prayers.
The One Who is More Than Being filled his soul
with nothingness no intellect could perceive
except the one that formed it in the first place.
He spilled his mind into the mind of God.
Visions of women in nothing more than towels
bent to anoint him. Grabbing at the oars,
he pulled the sea back over what he had prayed.

The Atonement

On into spring, around St Anselm's day,
I take another look at the Redemption,
and first I ask, What is there to redeem?

What have I done but fall into this flesh
which is the way it is because it is
and not because of something someone did

to That-Than-Which-None-Greater-Can-Be-Conceived—
which is a phraseology I admired
and admired Professor Quinn for saying it

the spring of '62 in that lecture hall
with casement windows hung on the musky breeze
bloody and bosomy and rank with love

and not God's love but Beverly Doherty's
who drove men mad on her front porch in the lamplight
to be at one with parts of her she kept

untouchable behind her father's door
shutting out all but the last smell of her
under the nostril in the sweet night air.

The Light of the Living

Trying to see the work of the eye
in what the eye was trying to see,

I went to where my eyes were,
where the inmost eye in the middle of me

looked out and found the sun on fire.
Birds fell from the sky like freezing rain.

Though it was summer, deep summer, deep
indolent summer, ice fell off treelimbs

breaking into pieces in thunder; then,
sooner than I expected, spring came—

intimate, comely, viridescent spring;
and so I strayed off into the air.

Two blind black angels hungry for home
climbed from the corners of my eyes.

The Monks at Large

There was a life outside of this one, which
the Old Ones told us was the one that was.
Guidance came freely but was often wrong.
Then mischievous Brother Malachy observed
that the greatest obstacle to godliness
worth breeching was the buckle at the waist
of a girl like Nora Doyle in Cornavogue.
Sniggering at that against our better judgment,
we nonetheless felt sure the man was right.
Where did it say there wasn't someplace else
for men to meet the truth that made them free?
If lives like ours were even feasible
to start with—if the keepers of the Faith
would keep it, were there any faith to keep—
we could have had good reason to take up
this type of work, if work was what this was.
Meantime, outside the wall, a pair of magpies
tumbled above the ditch along the road.
We stood to watch them. Father Bernard begged
the Mother of Christ to shut her face from us,
as we stepped out down a path of mottled shade
into a field of girlish marigolds.

The Queen of Heaven

His craving for the flesh of Mary Quinlan
had faded softly into dumb disuse.
Now and again he walked down the boreen
beside her cottage in the aspen copse,
and he could draw up from his soul the dream
of moss as bright as ginger among her thighs
where he could leap like a great frog after a rain.
The way in was a low path under branches,
and there were nettles in the ditch beside,
but Mary Quinlan sang to the sweet winds
that nudged the curtains at the kitchen window
where he might see her shadow in the lace
or take her song and carry it on his way
up to the bridge to croon it to the river.
A gang of blackbirds bickered from the poplars.
One Friesian uttered forth a burst of spray,
blessing the buttercups. He kept on singing.
The sound rose like a noise among the nations,
a lovecry from the heart's embitterment,
the loin's remorse for sweetness kept away,
where grey walls showed the Virgin and her child
a blue fly on the lampshade by the bed.

A Creak of Hinges

Night after night I dreamed about hotels,
mostly the same one, with a thousand rooms,
in one of which I left all of my clothes
and in another someone that I loved,
while in a third my own distracted self,
whose odd persona I had never met,
was looking for a way to take a shower,
facing a rack of suits in an old armoire
that I imagined was a shower stall,
with a woman entering from the fire escape
to find her husband underneath the bed
while this demented man who stared at her
from behind the shivering door of an old armoire
was only looking for a decent room
somewhere around this dull arrondissement
at one of any number of plain hotels
that cater to backpackers or wayward priests
on holiday with young girls from the parish
or men like him in search of who knows what
that leads them into streets with grey façades
and double doors revealing passageways
emptying into courtyards where cupids leap
on one foot over bursts of pearly spray
besprinkling the sun's imperial countenance.

Free Country

Invite them in to where they take you over,
any of them who happen to have seen
the way you looked askance at them, enough
to mind it. They were only too well aware
of dissolute black corners in the cellars
of your gelatinous depravity, complete
with cobwebs and milky drool. Custom holds,
in these parts anyhow, that who one knows
means everything, but only if
the priests determine that a holy wind
fondled the top fronds of the bristlepalms
at the exact moment of that person's birth
you sought the aid of, under flights of swans.
You gave me words I would have loved to have
for my support group, or the ladies in
the Lyric Relief Guild, home-truths more poignant
and more rife with wild complaint
than the usual mindfuck. A tropical brightness
sweltered and grew thin. Trouble that fell
on everyone was all one kind of trouble.
At least we knew we were supposed to know that
and to try to do something to take care of it,
even on such an abject afternoon
in the middle of any number of broken lives
mended by all the good word we could get
to filter through to us over assumed names.

The Banquet

A hallway bigger than most people's houses
awaited me in the next to last episode.
At the end of it a massive double door
opened on the Duke of Tuscany at table
attended by naked dwarves. I stayed outside
to watch the evening play through the draperies
at the farther end of the hall where I came from,
with its enormous doorways quiet as caverns.
I knew there were councillors in the anteroom
full of news even I could deliver with aplomb,
but the lord was at table in the midst of his joy,
made much of, whispered to, kept in regard
by persons whose bodies fed from his own.
Behind me other doors were wobbling shut.
I knew if I walked in to where the great man was,
my soul no longer would be mine to save.
Glory and madness dwelt in the one room.
The way my shoulders turned when I looked back
was like a wall that stood behind my eyes
and echoed with the good loud noise I made.

Lost Boy

He wrapped a hand around my right forefinger
and walked with me down the hill to the bus stop
by a broad boulevard under aching light.
We stepped inside a house with tinted windows.
Women in bathrobes moved from room to room.
A bus was coming down a corridor.
I left him waiting there and went back out
into the sunlight and on up the street
where I could see a prospect of the city
verging toward purple hills and turquoise sky.
A cul-de-sac in the shadows to one side
invited me down to the doorsill of an inn.
The air hung thick with essence of lavender
among egret feathers in the cool vestibule.

The innkeeper's wife ran in from the dining room
and turned around once on her tiny heels.
She saw me from the middle of her turn.
I was explaining how unblameworthy I was,
since all I came for was to find my way
out of this place, nice as it happened to be,
and pleasant as all my memories ever after
would certainly seem to my clear inner eye,
though all I wanted now was a route of egress
by some means through that back wall over there,
so I could take my leave and make my way
back up the hill I came down earlier,
leaving my mother at the restaurant
with ivory fingers folded on the table.

The Music of Forgiveness

I can't believe I am telling this again.
When he came back that night, he had a load
of answers, as he put it, and he knew
why I was angry with him that whole time.
He walked in with a wild look in his eye,
wilder than any I had ever seen,
on him or anybody, drunk or sober;
and he was mainly sober, though with a look
and with a way of lunging through the door
as if he had been pushed in by some thing
that stood behind him in the dark outside.
He said he got here in one piece, the way
I told him he would have to if he came home;
and he had not been drunk, more than halfway,
before I found him as I found him then,
trembling and weeping, rubbing at his face
with both his wrists, both of them slick with tears
and shoved out from the sleeves of his good coat
so his elbows almost popped through at the cuffs;
and in the midst of this he was telling me
he hadn't any right to anyone's
forgiveness, and the things he spent his life
doing to me were unforgivable.
I wished I knew what he was getting at
or what he'd done to me that was that bad.
Later that week I saw the last of him.
We sat at the far end of the Fifth Floor
away from all the others—for his sake:

he said he was embarrassed, still, to be there.
Everything had at last come clear to him:
he had written down the answers he came home with
in a book about my anger—how my anger
was the power that drove the planets around the sun,
and he had come to be in tune with it,
he said, which was the reason why he hummed
so much, and bothered people with his humming—
he understood that now, but couldn't stop;
and so the last thing that I heard him do
was hum whatever melody that was—
if it was even music—that he hummed
and kept on humming. I can hear him now,
the way I always hear him when I tell you this.

Manchild

Green thickets hiding me from all but joy
or night alarms that raised me up too far
toward enmity against particular
embodiments of the everlasting Why
left me at last with slumber in a dry
confusion. Thunder, birdsong, rainfall were
divine ideas of an earlier
redemption in the skin. I was a boy
of seven underneath. Multiple sins
against the sacred idiom of desire
cried out to be expunged. This joy I mention,
it was like candy-drops in little tins,
like tiny coals nesting inside the fire,
the look of larks taking a turn in sunshine.

What did you mean by that, madman? Whatever
it ends up saying is the thing I mean.
I mean to say precisely what the lover
says when he finds beloved words again
to make beloved talk for his beloved.
Nobody's reason for the things I do—
as I continue moving in the vivid
kingdom the likes of me can hardly know—
bears any likeness to the things I see.
You call it what you will—call it insane—
call it a temperamental vanity
of heart and head—call it the utmost sign
of something rampant in the poor man's soul
and ugly as a rat in a sewer hole.

But these were larks and these were elms as well
and tulips yellow, pink and lavender,
and here were squirrels facing each other
around a plumtree by the garden wall
and yes, I kept on thinking, yes, of all
the other lovely things to tell to her
including certain wonders that never were
except in nightsongs once the quiet fell
and I could listen to the silences
between words, where the words were hidden fast.
And when this knowledge came on me at last
that she might hear me if I said she was
the one bad woman that I ever knew
worthy of praising, maybe that would do.

But what is this you're up to, madman, now?
But me no buts, Alonzo, said the Friar
in green organza riding his gravid cow
with gaudy yellow horns that read DESIRE
on banners purply curling from them both.
One might do worse than ride a cow's backside,
crowed joyous Harry unfolding his face beneath
two eyes that roamed a virginal forehead
winsome and white as lily-petals fallen
upon a lawn where languid ladies strayed.
Let me be lethal, let me be sullen,
the captious Captain bragged: Nobody lead
the likes of us till I arise and come
from the holy city of Delirium.

Nobody knows the trouble that came then.
It wasn't long before I rose and went
and left behind the scent of all that pain
and sped to find that cubby in a tent
of hedgerows leaning green and difficult
beside a yard where other children sat
by toys their stranger mothers found no fault
to let them play with, and I looked at that
thin strip of grass between the dirt and walk.
There came some footsteps falling, and I saw
a lady wearing lady-clothes. Her talk
was plain: Boy, she said, if you do not know
the one thing that I told you, listen again:
Learn to disdain the things that want disdain.

I got up toward the breaking of the day
to take my bearings from that broken dream,
but all the streetlamp gave me was a room
much like the one I slept in as a boy,
except the buses didn't run all night
and there weren't any ships braying upriver.
Out where the planets were was dark as ever
for all my lack of motive to look out
and wonder anymore. Whatever they said
was there I took for granted, what was not
was not, and what a man could do I did
about the things I had some say about.
Anything much else was in the mind of God,
even the daybreak, what there was of it.

Great Beast

I dip a hand for snakes known to these weeds
to writhe around the floor beside my shoe.
Desperate enmities between a man
and lower forms of life should flake away.
Anytime anyone the way I am
could understand what I have understood,
the matter of continual aplomb
facing the air and lifting into it
one foot beside the other with a brow
stuck forward at the coming circumstance
should never be a thing one took for granted.
Outside my window there, the grumbling crows
await their turns to take the air again
to tear it with their nasty blasphemies
and put it back together as a veil
of rags that wag and dangle in the breeze
their oily cries contaminate. The bird
I'd like to be if I could be a bird
would hiss and bark and curse at the same time,
a kind of man and crow and watersnake
with ragged wings that flapped but did not fly.

The Rendering

Early in the winter of the year 1312, the monks of the Cistercian abbey of Fossanuova took the body of Thomas Aquinas, who had died there in March of 1274, and boiled the flesh from the bones, in order to place them in a small casket that could be moved from hiding place to hiding place, so great was their fear of the Dominicans of Toulouse, the brethren of Thomas Aquinas, and so deep was their love for the Angelic Doctor, who had chosen this monastery as the place to die, giving them the right, so they thought, to keep his bones forever in their care. A quantity of flesh remained, after all those years, since Thomas Aquinas had been a corpulent man, who had died in the odour of sanctity. A first unearthing of the corpse, by these same jealous Cistercians, for the purpose of moving it to a place of greater seclusion, revealed the corpse to be still incorrupt. When they took the remains up out of the chapel floor, a sweet air spilled forth from under the coffin lid. On that occasion, the abbot James of Ferentino appointed three monks to exhume the body and decapitate it. The head was placed in a metal box and immured in a corner of the chapel. A time afterward, in the early winter of the year 1312, both head and trunk were boiled. The monks prepared two cauldrons for the purpose, one for the severed arms and legs of Thomas Aquinas, along with the head from its metal box in the chapel, and the other for the great mass of gut and heart. The left hand had already been removed, in 1288, by Aquinas's sister, the Countess Theodora of Sanseverino, whereas the right thumb had been taken, shortly after death, by Aquinas's secretary and companion, Reginald of Piperno. The boiling took place behind the chapel, in the monastery courtyard, in the open air, a few paces in the direction of the pigsty. The steam that lifted in billows to the ashen sky carried in it an aroma like that of seasoned venison. One of the attending monks later claimed that he had indeed placed two large sprigs of finochio in the bubbling cauldrons. An oily vapour breathed lightly over the cheeks of the monks around the cauldrons as they rubbed their elbows against the early winter chill. An old monk marching briskly through the courtyard on his way to Vespers took a deep breath and muttered something about the lavishness of the fare being prepared for the abbot's table. Monks wearing sturdy leather gloves pushed staves against the cauldrons and upended their contents onto the ground. The bones were allowed to cool, and were then gathered into a crate and carried into the rear of the sacristy. What was left of the flesh was buried at the site where the cauldrons had stood. A cat came stepping out from the monastery's grain bin to poke her nose where the juice of Aquinas lay soaking in the earth among cinders and clods of clay. From his place near the pigsty Brother Bonifacio watched as the cat's tongue lapped at an islet of fatty film on one of several puddles. Brother

Bonifacio lifted a pitchfork from its peg. He took the pitchfork in both hands. He crouched up carefully behind the cat. Just as she raised her head to lick the smudge from the hairs of her upper lip, the monk pushed the pitchfork between her shoulders.

Summer in Umbria

I used to sit down drunk on my front porch
to watch the afternoon and the mulberry

mingle together with timbrels and dances
to the windchime's ruthless tinkle, as if the sun

could leap and kick his heels around that tree
in her small gown of green, beside the shadow

because it was not the light I wanted there,
but other light that stood among cypresses

beyond a garden with figtrees and cicadas
jangling above the voices of young girls

who stopped to take their shoes off by the gate
so they could dance home barefoot from there on.

The Ape of Emain Macha

The king at Emain Macha had an ape
which someone brought to him from Africa.
This was a Barbary ape, whose skull was found
when the great mound was opened, along with brooches,
trumpets, other bones of pigs and cattle—
nothing unusual, except for the ape's skull,
and a man's skull, also, severed down the middle.

I lay on top of that great dome over Ulster,
and watched two blackbirds drifting near the sun.
They made a pair of rings one on the other.
I heard the roar of the king's boy-warriors
striving with Cuchulain on the Armagh road.
The king's ape leaped and screamed with terrible joy
to see the blood of children spilt for fun.

A Highway Brook in Dingle

Travelling the coast road from Ventry to Slea Head,
    we came to a place where the blacktop
stops by a brook rushing down from the mountain
    over stones replacing the highway,
providing us both miracle and hazard,
    with a thought for the County Council
and how they could countenance such a marvel—

as well as a thought for the cliff's edge just there
    to one side of us, frighteningly
hidden by the roadside wall and swollen turf.
    We scarcely thanked God for good weather.
Mist would at least obscure the terrible plunge.
    We had no choice but to go on through.
Halfway over, we stopped and opened the doors

to pick up glistening stones for souvenirs.
    The rattling water from above us
had come to be under us, and below us
    the ocean murmured as oceans do.
Old gods might be staring from behind the light
    at this intersection of known worlds,
while the human roadway rose to carry its fare.

The Moving Statue at Melleray

The Virgin stood alone in her shady niche
and would not move, although the light would move
among the rhododendrons, seeming to touch
her form with rippling spots of pink. Above,
the sun looked very lively, but the lady
kept herself quiet, with her palms together,
a ring of stars over her brow, her body
muted under the gown she wore, or rather
that someone carved her in. A loud man prayed
ahead of seven others at their prayers,
all of them groaning in the greenlit glade
about their sins and keeping away from fires,
but Mary made no motion. Water spilled
from a pipe into a pool that was black and cold.

Poulnabrone Dolmen

They buried the old king under this capstone
after they carved his brain out with a shell
and broiled the rest of him. They wrapped his bones
in elkskin, once the god devoured his soul
and the druids had eaten his brain uncooked,
passing the bits among them on a stick.
They covered the burial under a mound of earth
which gradually disappeared, leaving these stones
with absolutely no sign of a man at all.
When I drove down here once, around midsummer,
I found a great rock bird about to fly,
until I noticed pools of recent rain
all over the capstone, while the one wren
that had come to drink took off into the country.

Lake Isle

There was in the likelihood of being charmed
by purple shadows over the still water
and the curlew's cry across it from the island
with its black remnant of a tower wall
subsiding near a few ministerial elms
a risk I knew I faced all on my own
under a sky releasing whiffs of breeze
that cooled my brow and loosed the thought of home
like a waftage of lavender from dresser drawers
opened by fingers I had dreamed of kissing
the morning there were voices in the hedge
and a pathway wandering into the garden's heart
the cry of whose one bird would make a shadow
that fled like a wintry call over black water.

A Catch in the Breath

Once I had found my way out of Dublin
one grimy Friday afternoon at rush hour,
I came to Kilkenny with its steamy fields
and Tipperary under a choking haze,
having passed by the Rock of Dunamase
just off the mainroad I was driving on,
where I might rest my back against a stone
and dream about the wood-owl's darkening call
across the valley from the aspen grove.
A wave of blackbirds rose up to a wire
and settled in a row. I came to Cashel,
giving the Rock of Cashel half a look,
then drove to Cahir to the Cahir House Hotel
and took a room on the top floor well above
the rattle and roar of lorries in the square,
along with the noise of the band in the ballroom
which the deskclerk told me would play that night,
and probably loudly, to a late hour.
I said I wouldn't mind it, being tired,
intending to get to bed more or less directly,
which I did not do. Instead, I walked around,
and stopped to watch a heron in the Suir,
beside the Castle, stepping carefully
among the stones, oblivious of me
or even of the traffic on the bridge,
till I succumbed to hunger like the bird's
and bought myself a bag of fish and chips
to dine on while I walked around the square.

I threw the paperbag in a trashcan
and walked up to the menubox by the door
of the Galtee Inn, to see how much the nightlife
could cost a man in Cahir. I went inside.
The barmaid was a girl I thought I knew
eleven years ago, and there she was,
lifting glasses by the rim three at a time
over the same bar she played under as a child,
ducking among the lunchcrowd on their stools.
One of the forms of grace we learn about
involves the avoidance of nostalgia
and other mysticalities men are given to,
making them stop and stand and rub their arms
with a lost look as if the feast were done
and the last guest were rising to go home.
If anyone was watching, it might have seemed
that that was what I did for a small time
standing to one side, till it came to me
that no one in the room, including her,
would care that someone all but lost in joy
had walked in out of the evening to stand there
among townspeople other than his own
taking a weekend's ease. As I walked out,
though there was light enough to see her by,
the heron had found a new place in the riv ▪.

A Girl Sings to Moravia at the World's End

Moravia appeared on Inishmore
one sunlit evening with his entourage—
two women and a glib photographer.
It was an odd place for Moravia.
The girls at Bridget Hernon's came to the gate,
as I walked up from the sunset at Bungowla,
to tell me Alberto Moravia had arrived,
and he was in the parlour beside the fire,
being sung to by a village girl in Irish,
with his silver-handled cane beside his knee,
under Oscar Wilde's grandfather's portrait
with the same chin and forehead as Oscar Wilde's,
as Bridget Hernon pointed out to us
while stirring coals and setting some turf in
for what appeared to be a bad turn in the weather
according to the forecast on the TV,
as well as a lost chance for Moravia
to see Dún Aengus, which the photographer
had no idea was only a short walk away,
a few fields up the hill behind the house,
though altogether beyond Moravia's
bad legs and ventricles. The girl's keening song
rose sharply on the warm air of the room.
After the silence came when she was done,
we all said "Brava" but Moravia,
who tapped the silver handle of his cane,
shaped to resemble a waterbird of some kind
with a long beak like a gull's or a cormorant's

and a half-smile like the one Moravia gave
instead of "Brava" for the girl's heartbreaking song,
the gist of which she tried to explain to us,
and the photographer, who had good English,
passed this along to Moravia, who nodded
and blinked his eyes under his great eyebrows,
but said precisely nothing in reply.
The girl began to sing another song,
that came from a joke the kelpers used to tell
in the 18th Century. She didn't know
the point of it herself, but she liked to sing it
because it had a lovely leaping tune,
and when she finished it, we all said "Brava,"
while Moravia wrapped his hand around the beak
of the silver gull or cormorant and moved his cane
in what seemed another gesture of approval,
except this time he pulled himself to his feet,
bent in a kind of wavering bow to us,
nodded his head to the girl, and left the room.
One of the women turned to me and said,
"Alberto is very tired." Bridget came back
to pick up the tea-things and to make it known
that the purple sunset meant fair weather tomorrow,
despite the television's foul prediction.
I said I hoped Signor Moravia
at least could see Dún Aengus, from a distance,
if not go up to it. I knew a boreen
off the main road south of Corrúch near Oatquarter
that led along the north side of the ridge
until Dún Aengus came into plain view,

but the boreen was rocky, and besides
I liked the way it seemed to belong to me
the afternoon I'd found it and gone down
to where Dún Aengus suddenly was there,
looking about to slide into the sea,
across the valley among choughs and bees.
The Italians all were on their way to bed.
They had brought Moravia to the world's end,
but could not carry him to the edge of it
to lean above the wailing kittiwakes,
for one last look at the long drop out of here,
or to tighten his hold around a waterbird
that would lead him back to listen beside the fire.

Magpies

My friend has come home from a week in Lourdes
between treatments at the Cork Cancer Hospital.
She says it's wonderful what they're doing now
to keep us all alive. But something always
is out for us, don't you think? she wonders,
waiting to get us, I mean, don't you think?
Sadness surprises me as I watch her hands
lifting her thought in the air and letting it go
like a magpie leaping a ditch into a meadow.
Through the window behind her a quick light shines
among elderberry bushes with their lacy disks
turned to the wolfpack sky above the vale.
Pastoral, she says, this place is a pastoral place,
the way we used to imagine the afterlife.
But there is no afterlife, she tells me then.
Even in Ireland, we have doubts about all that.
We live here now; and afterwards, most likely,
the magpies come to leap over the ditches.

The Land of Heart's Desire

Eriugena caught the sound of God
coming to him one night from a lost moon
that hid itself behind a drumlin wood
not long before the sun came back again.
This was the music light makes over Ireland,
as jackdaws toss themselves like chips of slate
over grey lake water under a smear of sky,
their cursive wingbeats writing nothing down.
Maybe he thought this was the song God made
the night the moon came out for the first time
to put light in the place of that much sky
that otherwise was dark without the moon.
All this is set forth in a book he wrote
in the 9th Century for the king of France,
who never understood a thing he meant,
but sat and drank and watched the moon go down
just before cockcrow, a long way from Ireland.

The Back Road to Arcadia

The tiny thought that breached the inner tissue
of a brain beleaguered as mine was
said that the other world could be drawn in
from the dream inside the neighbourhood,
which was the same kind of dream as the ones
that flicker through a man's mind at night,
regardless of all that daybreak with its birds.
Then the tree chirped and the light grew thin.
The backs of paving stones were black as beetles.
I had come by the back road to Arcadia.
Pin oaks and mimosas held up redbuds by the arms.
A pair of grackles scraped the sky and plummeted.
Dogpen yapped to dogpen. Forsythia
splattered the white wall of the toolshed.

A Light in the House

Nobody seems to know what Jesus meant.
At least not me. I let the cat come in
to eat her dinner by the stereo
where Ashkenazy bends to his andante.
He seems to know exactly what Mozart meant.
The cat looks glad to have these bits to eat,
these keys of mercy struck above her ears
which tremble unbeknown at what they hear.
God knows I'm happy too, I know I am,
though nobody seems to know what Jesus meant.
I know I don't. I am compelled to watch
and listen here, more mystified than ever,
and not for lack of trying, even though
the pool of daylight by the cat's backside
or the quiet after Vladimir quits the keys
brings more beatitude than I could bear.

Midsummer Light as the Soul's Habitat

It wasn't the turnings of appearances
nor any of their exactions from the air
that made me think the afternoon was bees
or gangs of bears in rowdy robes of fur.
I hadn't thought of this for any reason,
and this wasn't anyplace but my back yard.
Here was the flavour of an illusion
that stuck to my tongue like a hummingbird
beating its wings into a blur of hunger—
one of those tones from the soul's undergrowth
where animals devoid of any anger,
taking up bits of countryside in their teeth,
can turn to look around them where they are
and shake their faces into shreds of fire.

The Nightgown

Once Wordsworth dreamed he met a Bedouin
bearing a spear and, under one arm, a stone,
which the Bedouin said was Euclid's *Elements*.
A shell took the spear's place, and then became
an emblem of something soothing to the spirit,
but Wordsworth couldn't tell about the stone
or why it had become some kind of book,
though soon he woke in a seacave with *Don Quixote*
open beside him, so Wordsworth said: "I see!
This shell is my prophetic Self; the stone
suggests a windmill grinding; I raise my spear
of poesy to strike against the mind's
impairment of the soul. I am the Bedouin,
the desert is the sea I slept beside
to dream this mighty dream." Later in Paris,
he slipped the button loose from the third hole
in the bodice of the nightgown Annette had on
one sultry night during the Revolution,
while the heavy spear he bore between his loins
presented itself to the shell she held in hers,
till all the other buttons tore loose and clattered
onto the floor like pebbles by the sea.
Then Wordsworth remembered the Bedouin, and saw
in one delirious spot of time on fire
a figure like a god astride the sunset
with a man before him prostrate, looking down
to where a broiling wheel throbbed in his eyes
and the smell of his own sweat steamed up from the dune,
which was her breastbone glistening under him.

Reading Aquinas

Maybe what Thomas means when he says grace
is its own prerequisite, or words to that effect,
has something to do with these sweet tides of joy
one feels now and then in the bottom of the breast
while crossing the street against the light
or watching children at play or cats copulating
or birds leaving the branches quivering under them
and the stillness of the branches afterwards.
Maybe it's times like these that Thomas means,
though I am in doubt on this and other issues,
including the one correlative idea
about how the Divine Essence cannot be known
to a person who is still in the body, except
"in dreams or alienations of the senses,"
which is a truly wonderful consideration
coming from a corpulent 13th-century Dominican—
and grace again is an explicit component here:
"the images in the imagination are divinely formed,"
involving "the infusion of gratuitous light,"
Thomas having elsewhere carefully explained
how it takes grace to prepare oneself for grace,
as in that sudden shower one afternoon last summer,
like a sparkling airy essence of divine light,
I found a portly African in a Hawaiian shirt
baptising himself in the street and marvelling:
"I couldn't help myself! This rain is exquisite!"—
the two of us finally standing face to face,
one of us an angel in a shirt of flowers,
the other blessed as he could be because of that.

Mud on a Boot

If by way of nuances known only to fluent minds
it becomes possible to see the idea in the middle,
whereby we turn and browse like animals
at ease in the day, I'd say that's good. You too
would say that's good. But once I looked
through a shutter into a street at an hour before dawn,
soundless except for a stray nightbird's reticent refrain
and the odd cascade of footfalls leaving off,
while subtler intimations divulged themselves
piecemeal; it was then you woke
and sat up in the bed and put both palms down flat
and looked first one way then the other
then the first way again, until you seemed to see
what it was you had awakened to look for,
out of some corner of your dream, and then you said
words I have not remembered, spoken regardless
in a highpitched piping tone
like that of the old woman who cleaned our room,
and when I heard that sound I could not breathe.

The shadow on the left side of the boy's nose
who was found that morning sitting in the café
put the right side of his nose in silvery brightness
for just the one moment that he raised his face
and welcomed us and offered us two chairs
at the table where he sat, and promptly got up
to busy himself about our morning meal. I could tell
your reluctance to converse derived from something
far away. Tendencies to fall into silence

came often between us from your side. I had even begun
to be halfway capable of the consciousness
of my own evident fecklessness in your eyes,
so it was not impossible for one part of my head
to say to another part: "She not only thinks
I'm an idiot, she *knows* I am." The same feeling
came over me this morning as I climbed the slippery stile
into the river meadow where I had gone
in search of brown trout under a bridge
a few miles west of town. Midstream the water,
swollen by recent rains, toiled through weeds and rocks.
My boots brought mud up from the river's edge.
I could see myself impaled on the steel fence-post,
slipping onto it from the 2x4
on top of the stile; what was left of me
would dangle in a tatter of denim rags,
maybe for days. The sheriff
would shake away the grin from his remark:
Some people never get it right.

The thought of being thus taken away
before my heart had filled enough with you
has kept me from one sudden consequence
after another all these many years. There was a bird,
as well, that clamoured under the bridge
among the piers, and that bird's cry
was a piping cry like one you made one morning,
for no reason I have yet to ascertain,
that was like the shrill noise of a crone,
the way she laughed to herself and shook her head
as we stepped down the hall at an odd hour.

Lawn Mower

When I came out on the far end of the swath
exposed by the 5-blade push-reel lawn mower
I had aimed in one direction till it reached
the fence that keeps my yard from my neighbour's woods,
I stopped and looked around at the green sea
with its wake of cuttings, and I asked myself
Why would you want to do a thing like that?
and then I stood the mower against the fence
and walked back up the path to the garage
where the boxes on the shelves along one wall
kept magazines and toys and hand-me-downs
and the open sack of cow manure on the floor
held promise of more grass I would not mow
and on the windowsill the radio
played Copland's "Fanfare for the Common Man"
amidst a rubble of wirenuts and flathead screws.

Angelology

When Robert Grosseteste comments on the angels
and whether more than one might coexist
in the same place or body, he seems to think
such fine points are important because they test
the seriousness of our preoccupations,
in this case with the business of the spirit,
of spirits generally, and the spirit of God.
The main idea posits medial forms
between God and ourselves, and furthermore
appropriates the model of the soul
as mover of the body, coextensive
as the body and the soul appear to be,
supposing here the soul's reality,
which was hard to question in the 13th Century,
though equally impossible to prove,
yet Robert argues the relationship
of angels to material elements
as casually as a man walking his dog,
showing us angels everywhere at once,
numberless angels all over the place
impinging on this world from the other world,
as the eye receives a vision of bare trees
mantled with mist, or the nostrils catch the savour
of a loved woman's delectable inner thigh
from mounds of mown grass in a stranger's yard.

Blackbirds

Coming in from watering the pepper plants,
I watch blackbirds descending from the roof
onto the cat's bowl by the mock orange tree.
They leap and peck at morsels and shake their heads
one at a time like bickering theologians
back in the days of the great heresies
troubling the Empire with anathemas
and disputations over syllables—
homoousion versus *homoiousion*—
one morpheme bringing in the Visigoths,
Alaric and Adolphus and the rest,
delivering Rome itself to frightful plunder.
Honorius, the sitting emperor,
survived a dozen years to sport the purple
while the Empire's fabric "yielded," in Gibbons' words,
"to the pressure of its own weight," weakened within
by murmuring monks and blear-eyed visionaries.
Mommsen would say it was slaves raiding granaries
provoked by water in the Spanish mines
or madmen belching fire and oracles.
At this point, seasonably, I give it up
and head on in to catch the Nightly News
for a homeopathic dose of *mal du siècle*,
but on the way I look up at the blackbirds
back on the roof. They have these looks that say:
We know exactly what is happening—
we know exactly who for Christ's sake we are.
I hope the cat's revenge is merciless.
I think I could turn and live with vegetables,
they are so savoury and unperplexed.

Watering Impatiens

Looking up as if to ask heaven for signs,
I noticed a blue as clean as a baby's sigh,
which I had known to expect, but even then
I only said I knew the things I saw,
and what I saw was empty of any signs,
as usual, which was itself a sign.
Whatever the vacant blue might be taken to mean
I left to colourists who cared for blue.
As for my own position under it,
flatly abstracted, with the neck bent back
to uphold a head pitched like a man-ape's skull
agog in the clay, I'd let anthroposophists,
those erstwhile friends who phone at 4 a.m.,
asseverate their notions, being as good
as any other cracked ideologues
at bringing truth to ground—it was all no more
than someone's name for someone else's fear
in an idiom no objection could gainsay.
What might be dangerous about such foolishness
was its capacity to win men over
to one immoderate claim on their convictions,
with no room left for any disbeliever.
My being here engaged in honest toil,
carefully hosing down the parched impatiens,
so they might raise their sweet parts toward the sun
in glorious disregard of all the above,
confirmed my place as love's apologist,
and emissary from the vegetation,
in the unending war against the sky.

Truth

Proust claimed truth is only a point of view
about things, which is as simple a refinement
on Augustine or Aquinas or Pascal
as anyone has come up with before or since.
This was a practical determination, entirely corrupt,
but far from theoretical or merely subjective.
Proust naturally had a novelist's motive
to get on with the story and to tell it well
from as many varying points of view
as he could imagine people to exhibit them.
Beyond that there was the esoteric
if not the theological aspect of it.
I wouldn't know much about either of those.
The truth is Proust couldn't know what the truth is,
certainly not now. And even in this life,
one of the few things he verified for sure
was the fact that one steeple viewed through the trees
has a different aspect from another steeple taken in
a few paces farther on up the lane,
which is your basic phenomenological program
given as a starting point in any history of ideas,
as well as an earthen vessel full of body waste
thoughtfully ingested by adenoidal pseudophilosophs,
whose ranks Proust was a micromillisecondth
of a braincell's fluctuation away from
on any given day. Heartbreaking as it is,
truth belongs only to someone positively unlike Proust,
who knew the paths of time and how they lead
past doors the dead would open if they could.

The Plan of Salvation

Whatever the reality, it is
a reality. The door isn't shut,
the door's open. That was Henry James's
word from a lady bound to die. And what
could be the least thing the matter with that
as an everyday attitude? One evening
in the spring of '64 the sunset broke
from a cloudbank like a great door opening
onto a golden room, and a voice spoke
words I took to be those of the lord God
on matters pertaining to the way things stood
for me and other mortals of my type,
or various issues he felt moved to take up,
none of which I remember at this time,
though it may be that the Everlasting then
and now was more of an impression I might form
in response to the way life seemed to be working out
or whatever occasions I might come upon
where the long range outlook was beyond my brain.
I hardly ever slept with the door shut.

A Canticle of the Stars

I wanted to walk outside and praise the stars
for lending me lights to look by in the dark.

I wanted to look at them and name their names
like names of angels flocking among the saints

to lift the saints up into the holy fire
where they could look like angels with their own eyes.

I wanted to walk upright in the real world
before the light took over and I was light

or the light's kinsman in the skin. I wanted
to walk awhile in the green place near the edge

where sweeter things than I was took up the light
into their kindly fingers and it was light

where they were. Before the light was all there was,
I wanted to walk around in the one world

once and for all, like other walking creatures
that made their way, taking up room in the dark,

striking the dark at both ends till they broke through
into the deep green space beside the waters

where dreamless beasts go quietly one by one
from light to shadow, nudging the dark aside

with their sweet faces. What could I do but look
and wipe my eyes? More gladness than I could stand

was all around me, and it was their doing
or so I kept on thinking back in my mind

until they looked to find me and there I was,
preparing to dance my dance in so much light

I might have ascended in a beam of it
among the angels rising into Christ's mind

while Christ was rapt in thinking about the sun
and how it writhes in fire for the likes of us.

Requiem

At the end of the millenium, in the city of the dream,
is a backstreet emptying into a square
dominated by a church whose façade consists
entirely of a mozaic of Christ Judging the Damned
among golden glitter catching the sunset
from the river opposite
where the street turns into an esplanade
along the lake with its villas and boatclubs

though I am searching for the dead friend I ate with
in a beanery downtown at a table with green chairs
beneath the grimy portrait of Our Beloved Founder
who, as a boy in Macedonia, watched from the rootcellar
the slaughter of his father, mother, and other townspeople,
before he left with one tapestry satchel
to come here to stare through astonished spectacles
over bins of hotdogs covered with damp towels

at Kovac and me eating two with everything
before we head off for the old man's funeral
where everyone gets up from a clatter of folding chairs,
the men smoking pipes, the women hugging their purses,
the children taking their places like good little soldiers,
the patriarch dissolving under billows of incense,
and Kovac's wire-rims flickering from the doorway
as he darts out into the noonday glare.

The Grotto

It began in a house with something wrong with it,
falling bricks and bursting water from the ceiling,
in the middle of the bikeride up Vernor Highway
toward the elusive Holy Places on the East Side
where the smokestacks of Detroit Edison were minarets
and cripples draped their deflated legs on the sidewalks,
begging endlessly for the end to come, for the light
to burst in us till we all glowed like lanterns.

It was 1965 in Paris on the Boul' Mich somehow,
sycamores in cages, whey-faced girls in white dresses,
an old woman in rags asleep on the sidewalk
with one palm upraised and a 5-centime piece in it,
big as a badge that said *Let me in, let me in, I'm with
the Ministry of the Poor, this is our dream.*
You people can move along now and head on home
and leave us our dream. In the shadows of the sycamores

it was later on that day in the old neighbourhood.
You wanted to argue that Mozart's brain
was no better than a superfine machine. Your point
was lost by the time we turned up the alley
with the little grotto in it where the Saint looked out
from behind his windowpane heaped with wilted sprigs
and candle-ends and two of his own shinbones
and the ivory ring bestowed on him by the Pasha.

The Night Breeze off the Ocean

It is heartrending to see them coming from such distances,
against so many difficulties: some of us try to help them
at least to reestablish themselves here in the manner
to which they had grown used. Once they learn
enough of the language to organise a daily routine,
and have discerned the dirtpaths into the mountains
where they can acquire that peace they yearn for,
it is more likely we can ignore them. Before they land,
the ship's engine whines for an instant and the great blade
reverses itself and grinds into the sea, as if to take them back.
Then the launch arrives, and they step onto it,
bobbing on the midnight water, lit around the edges
by only the few lights from cafés or hotels. Behind them shuts
the door into lost memories, the way it always does, the way
it did for us. One day we will tell them how
there is often a small beam leaking near the knob
which it is our duty to take in hand and turn.

*

What is beautiful here,
what is nicely proposed to the eye,
is the balance of light and shade
in consort with the harmony of useful
and useless objects, along
with a few in obvious disuse, as, say,
that shed over there beside
the fence which leads to the line
between a private residence
and the neighbourhood house of worship.
As mere observer, only by chance brought here
for no objective reason, out of the fray,
and as it happens watching children play,
I like the felicity of these things being here,
under these racing clouds across this stunning sky,
of a blustery afternoon in early March,
and in a certain tepid year already rushing by.

*

We should not consider God any more
than any other natural inclemency
the end of contemplating which will fulminate beyond itself
into high-flown undertakings for the soul to waste its time on
in place of other minor particulars
that could be called to its attention
far more profitably to the rest of us left here
in our perfunctory lives
no more than halfway known to anyone
beyond the immediate vicinity.
God is a principle of infinite incoherence
at one with other principles of tireless vengeance
against the corporeal vibrancies of the universe,
as is attested in the record. Likewise God
is known to lack integrity, and as for grace
God has no idea what that is. This is not the friend
one ought to seek for comfort at the end.

*

The afterlife is the past remembered
in the dreams of the dead. So I climbed to the top
of the rocky hill littered with whitewashed shrines; inside,
the coolness rushed onto my face, just in from the heat,
from the faces of saints in cracked blue robes on the walls.
Another time I went to relieve myself
behind a friend's cottage near the Atlantic
in County Clare, and the winds blew over a ditch
full of shimmering black water and bits of trash,
and the whole countryside rose up around me
like the inside of an upended crystal globe. And there I crouched
lifting the embattled face of Bertie Mahon
from the front page of the *Irish Independent*.
Those were among my life's indelible experiences, utterly unrelated,
the one involving an encounter with the sacred, the other
also involving an encounter with the sacred,
on both my part and that of Bertie Mahon.

*

Loose gruel was placed on the table in little plastic bowls
and we went to it breaking our fast with relish.
Maybelle sat in the corner under the open window
quietly peeling apples and slicing them for the porringer.
Magpies fled the oakwood in the distance.
Drawing the linen solemnly across his lips, Adrian rose to speak:
"My good friends, you have given much to be here.
I myself have wished it might be otherwise. Bear with me.
We are planning to take the means into our hands
to finalise a situation that should empower us all
in ways no one will feel other than completely happy with.
The King of the Gypsies is coming for dinner."
Some of us gasped. Maybelle stopped peeling. Crows called
from the windy tops of the cedars along the road.
As usual, I knew they were the voices of the dead
who spoke to us with more than ordinary poignancy
about what was coming to grief even now under our noses.

*

Maybe it was just then and no other time
that the sweetness came and filled us and gathered away
the part of us that warmed to it and became
full of so much delight the thought of it could linger
in a corner of our brains for the rest of our lives.
It may have been only a momentary illusion,
a fabrication of the perceptual apparatus,
and for that matter only for that instant
in the entire history of the psyche,
and in this peculiar embodiment,
with no one else's equal and apposite evidence
before or since. In order to disprove this,
I would have to go about the byways of the earth
to find some other who knew what I mean; for now,
it is enough to know that you were there
and could, if I could find you, confirm what I have said,
offering your own versions of the colours.

*

The upshot is everyone's collective wish
to see you gone. They let you know this way:
a lawyer writes to say he has a will to read
which you no doubt would profit from hearing.
When you arrive at the appointed time,
there is a crudely handlettered for-sale sign
leaning behind a crack in the front window
with strips of fading duct-tape over it.
On the desktop barely visible through the grimy pane
a Nehi bottle balances on top of a green Selectric II.
A screwdriver and a carpenter's rule hold two points
of a cobweb, with the other hanging from the bottle neck,
like the sail of a dhow off Zanzibar.
Which is where you are. All you could do was flee
to take a room in the Regency Hotel in Dar-es-Salaam
with the girl you met on the bus from Mwanza,
who will steal out onto the balcony beside you.

A Voyage to the Island

We sail there together. He resolves to stay.
I return home to marry and raise children.

My last son is a poet who, coming of age,
heads over to locate my old companion,

who long since, in the cool of his cave,
has come to satori. Up walks the last son,

seeking him out for what his father told him,
so he and the holyman set off for the hills

to receive certain visions. One afternoon
they witness the Buddha bending into himself

in the shape of a scorpion curling its tail
and eyeing them hour by hour amid the blazing day,

which drives them mad. Eventually they open a hotel.
I arrive for a visit, having failed at everything.

The Plight of the Old Apostle

It came to this, if it came to anything:
my brave ambition was adrift in heartache,
so that I winced and grumbled and tried to look
as if it unbecame my hardwon standing
as a higher form of life around this place,
but what it was that did this I could not tell,
though once or twice I got to the verge of it:
the thing hung in me in a great drape of steel
that boomed and rattled when I went to move,
like an onslaught of ugly weather that drove off
dogs and belongings and townsmen to high ground,
with a few loose papers tumbling the alleys,
a lost child lurching from corner to corner,
the churchbells chiming no one to services.
I stopped short of wondering where it would end
or for what reason I was suffering so—
I who had done no wrong in a life of toil
and whom the dread of ruin or sudden death
had never once bewildered with indolence.
What wore me down was not so much how to lift
this rusty stupor that was over my mind,
but how to get up alive in spite of it.
I nurtured a thousand possibilities.
The one I liked the best involved leaving town
and making myself master of a small cave
above the harbour on a whitewashed island
where the girls were shy but willing and the life
was easy as picking figs off the figtrees

that clung to the hills against a spotless sky,
and the bartenders all grinned when you sat down
and woke you with a drink after siesta.
Now this was the life I knew I'd like to live,
and come to find out it was this life I was
heartsick about—a life in another life
I might have dreamt of once on waking: a sky
so blue you went all blue walking under it
and your face turned glassy blue when you looked up
and the girls said nothing and hardly had to
because they knew you and you knew they knew you
and said so by the way they nodded toward you
or half smiled from the windowsills as you passed
beneath them, and one of them let down a grin
so wide you could step through it and disappear
into the teeming bramblebush of her brain—
a place so strange you lost your bearings in it
and came out on the other side wise and blind
and able to prophesy and aim the sails
of men ambitious after things men desire
and only the dead have lost ambition for.

Café Paradiso

A woman sits at a table by the wall.
The waiter brings a plate of octopus
and a beaker of cool wine. The air is full
of jasmine, and the woman's skin is sweet
as the flowers of jasmine leaning by her chair
from the potted bush beside it. Glorious
simplicity abounds in the sun's glare
from the wall her shadow seems to have stained
like the body's interruption of the mind
when the mind has begun to come upon the truth
about our ordinary lives on earth,
while here before it, in the least of places,
beauty is breathing in and breathing out
and watching the rest of us watching her
like so many imbeciles with dreaming faces.

Badia Fiesolana

No sooner had the blue air over the garden
become pearlescent in the spindly trees

than I perceived a cloud bank rolling in
to take me from a backroad near Fiesole

where my good friend and I went walking
with our walking sticks beside pastel villas

and we said the lovely women that we knew
must likewise find us lovely, though we were not,

and I could only imagine why God would make
these women crazy enough to love us the way they did—

two young men waxing old on our walking sticks,
two crazed swains lurching off along the road

to view the tombs in the Badia Fiesolana
and run our fingers over polished stones

that took our breath away and made us sigh out loud,
What is this love we carry to our graves?

The Disenthralled

Those blessed habitats around the yard,
where the braincells keep oddments of former lives,
can gleam with rare decorum, suddenly,
lifting you out of ordinary time,
so you can find out how you came to be here
where the mild old gentleman in the broad plaid coat
reached for a breath while hurrying up to give you
another recollection from the War,
hardly betraying the least canniness
about the world's way or his own life even,
itself for him merely an incident
in a series of discontiguous events
involving other men more praiseworthy,
which is the unavoidable inference
the mind absorbs from what he rubbed his jaw
to offer, seeming all the while a man
of customary breadth and easy wherewithal,
a veritable banquet of a human being,
though all left over, but for what he tells,
or thinks he does, of what he used to be,
until the fatal pause arrives to part you
releasing you to others, who will come
awash in afternoon bedazzlements
to pluck you from that region of the soul
into another where the day-lilies
pretend advanced conditions of aplomb.
It seldom ever is a different way.
After the last insouciant departure,

the scented air falls cool and affable.
A measured crunch of footfalls up the path
precedes the dreadful visitation:
almost as if a voice from the other side
had garbled messages to breathe to you,
you turn your ear intently toward the news
a man and woman strolling amiably
among the pale green shadows of the roadway
intimate barely audibly between them
before you note your own voice crying out.
Once, in what really was another time,
they were your fellow voyagers abroad,
gaining the corner by the Swan Hotel,
briskly materialising above cobblestones
among half-timbered shopfronts, gabled roofs,
the fabulous lost quarter at the end
of the last block in the town within a town
you always knew was there. A lambency
of afternoon suffused the white façade
of the cathedral, with its towers alike
except for billboards on the northernmost
extolling virtues various and timely
against a sky patrolled by silver birds
in tightknit teams of no more than five each
leaping in gusty bolts across the blue,
while herebelow a priest in overalls
and roman collar knelt to his flowergarden
beside the campanile, his forehead flecked
with glints of bloom. His mind was orchid-light
breaking upon the darkness he understood

as deity but never could divulge
to the immediate neighbourhood, so gave
his mind to bee and blossom, leaf and jay,
his broken heart consoled by lonely joy
of abject reckoning, while the comforter
visited someone else, he told himself,
if only to believe that this could be,
which was no small thing for the likes of him,
and as for that one who was comforted,
he prayed to learn from intercourse of spirits,
once they attained their mutual paradise,
what earthly bliss was like, if they had power
to recollect it from that timeless quiet
so like the calm that dropped from stopping bells
till pigeons lit along the ledge again
to peck above him poking at the ground.
The circumambulation of the soul
would have been like that, bringing to the heart
the rise of blood that comes from other life
discovered suddenly, the way you round
a corner to a place you knew of old,
the innkeeper and his young wife sitting down
to take a bit of brandy with the couple
who spent the whole day at the doll museum
in Winchester in a lane near the Cathedral.
It was the sadness in their eyes that haunted her,
their looks of frozen longing, while for him
it was the pathos in the way these people gave
their daughters little statues instead of love,
to touch our hearts in the next century

with dimpled fingers reaching from lacy sleeves,
their empty hands uplifted. Having said so,
he raised cigar and snifter in one fist
to catch the firelight like a leaping bird
or like a child's face crying from the glass
to be delivered. At the sight of that,
the four of them lapsed into silences
composed of memories unique to each,
the meaning of which was lost on one and all.
Fragrant with widowed aunts and morning-glories,
a gorgeous wildness kept its own domain
in the next block over. Patrick, the airedale,
tapped off along the hall toward the vestibule
to lie down with a shudder and a sigh,
an equilibrium having set in
so all were satisfied to be where they were
or to go elsewhere if it could be done
over an ocean of equanimity
covered with islands whose interiors
kept villages of corrugated roofs
and bougainvillea that the black goats browse
miles above captains in the anchorage.